Birth to Three in Education and Care:

Rudolf Steiner, Emmi Pikler, and the Very Young Child

Edited by Heather Church

Spring Valley, New York

Birth to Three in Education and Care: *Rudolf Steiner, Emmi Pikler, and the Very Young Child*

© 2022 Waldorf Early Childhood Association of North America

All rights reserved. No part of this book may be reproduced in any form without the written permission of the publisher, except for brief quotations embodied in critical reviews and articles.

ISBN 978-1-936849-57-4

Cover image: photograph by Megan Mumford

Published in the United States by

The Waldorf Early Childhood Association of North America
285 Hungry Hollow Rd.
Spring Valley, NY 10977
+1 845-352-1690
info@waldorfearlychildhood.org
www.waldorfearlychildhood.org

For a complete book catalog, contact WECAN or visit our online store at *store.waldorfearlychildhood.org*

Epigraph: Ruth Reardon, "How Do I Learn Just Who I Am?" In *Listening to the Littlest* by Ruth Reardon (Norwalk, CT: C. R. Gibson Co., 1984).

This publication is made possible by a grant from the Waldorf Curriculum Fund.

Contents

How Do I Learn Just Who I Am?................................. 5
   Ruth Reardon

Foreword 7
   Heather Church

Introduction 9
   Magdalena Toran

Profound Foundations: Waldorf Early Childhood
   Education and the Pikler Approach 13
   Susan Weber

Our Hands, Our Eyes, Our Voices: The Baby's Welcome 23
   Katherine Scharff

Understanding and Supporting Free Movement
   from Birth to Three 37
   Jane Swain

Caregiver Interactions with Infants and Toddlers
   During Diapering: Caregiver Responsiveness,
   Child Well-being, and Involvement 49
   Deborah Laurin, PhD

Recommended Resources 63

Contributors 65

Birth to Three in Education and Care

How Do I Learn Just Who I Am?

I learn from you who I am.
Within your eyes I see
reflected me.
Within your voice I hear
how you see me.
You are the mirror that I look into
and mold the image of myself.
I sense the way you hold me,
and from your touch
I feel my form, my shape.
And if I like what I see in
your eyes,
your voice,
your touch—
My heart responds and reaches out.
Then in its reaching, grows and grows,
until I see myself
as separate.
That separate self—in turn—
can love you back.
Because you taught me
who I am,
and I am loved.

Ruth Reardon

Birth to Three in Education and Care

Foreword
Heather Church

In this book you will find the wisdom of years of dedication to deepening the understanding of the child in the first three years of life. Each of the four lectures given by Susan Weber, Jane Swain, Katherine Scharff, and Debbie Laurin give a small view of the depth of understanding and the immense courage these four women have had to pioneer this work on behalf of Waldorf early childhood. It has been an honor to work together with these wise women to create the first birth to three conference and now a book publication. For many years we have been working to create a support network for parents, teachers, mentors, and teacher trainers on behalf of the young child and in support of Waldorf early childhood education. The four lectures deepen the connection and understanding of the work of Rudolf Steiner (1861–1925) and Dr. Emmi Pikler (1902–1984) and their intrinsic connection.

May this wonderful conference and publication be followed by many more.

Birth to Three in Education and Care

Introduction
Magdalena Toran

In October 2019, before any of us knew how much our lives would change in the coming years, there was an important gathering at Sophia's Hearth Family Center and Training Institute in Keene, New Hampshire. The first ever North American Birth to Three in Education and Care conference took place over the course of three days. Eighty participants came together to deepen our understanding of this most essential time in the life of a human being. We had our senses supported in the thoughtfully designed space that is Sophia's Hearth. We felt warmed by the care of the conference organizers and the faculty and staff who hosted our visit. Our bodies were nourished through beautiful, homemade food and each one of us was treated to care practices. It was a true festival.

A birth to three conference would have been enough cause for gathering, but that weekend also gave us an opportunity to celebrate another important moment: Susan Weber's retirement. Susan was *the* pioneer in the early days of birth to three. It was her will, alongside a few others, that literally birthed the birth to three movement in North America. To welcome her as a keynote speaker in the newly completed Sophia's Hearth building, which was the fulfillment of her vision for a Waldorf childcare and training center, was momentous indeed.

Susan Weber, birth to three educator and pioneer

This book shares its title with the theme of this conference: *Birth to Three in Education and Care: Rudolf Steiner, Emmi Pikler, and the Very Young Child.* Debbie Laurin, Katherine Scharff, Jane Swain, and Susan Weber gave the keynote addresses. These colleagues have devoted their life's work to understanding the young child, to what the child's needs might be, and how we, as conscious adults, can welcome them most warmly into their physical bodies, onto their paths as human beings. We, in the Waldorf early childhood movement, are deeply fortunate to have such wise, thoughtful, courageous, loving people as forerunners of the work with young children in North America. Each of these women has been deeply influenced by the insights of Rudolf Steiner and the work of Emmi Pikler. They have helped show how these two remarkable people, through different paths of inquiry, came to many of the same understandings about young children. This book is a collection of the keynote lectures given over the course of that birth to three conference weekend. They are deeply inspiring, encouraging, and hope-bringing.

Our colleagues, through their own practices based on the wise insights of Emmi Pikler and Rudolf Steiner, reminded and reinspired us to approach our work of caring for young children with deep interest. Over the course of three days, we were reaffirmed in our conviction that every time we interact with a child there is a meeting between two people, and this meeting has a powerful effect on the child's physical, emotional, and soul/spiritual well-being. Together we explored anew the welcoming power of respectful, caring relationships as great invitations into our bodies, which are our homes while we are here on earth. We were encouraged to pay attention to the quality of our voice, to the language we choose, and how this helps to orient the child. We were brought into greater awareness of how slowness in our speech and gestures is essential for the child's well-being and ability to process all that they are taking in. Powerfully, in each lecture, we returned to freedom of movement and healthy relationships. Freedom of movement is the key to healthy development and a child's lifelong capacity to become themselves; healthy relationships are built through presence, attention, deep listening, conscious touch, and careful observation, rooted in the knowledge that when we care for a child's physical body, we are in a shared process together—a dance of respect and interest.

In her keynote, Susan Weber spoke of *Wayfinding* by M. R. O'Connor, which researches indigenous methods of travel and navigation. Wayfinding—what a powerful term. Is it not what all of us are doing? Is it not what we are hoping to support the children in our care to do? I would say that wayfinding is also what brought these women to find the work of Rudolf Steiner and Emmi Pikler. In her book, O'Connor acknowledges that indigenous peoples have profound relationships with their landscape, allowing them to navigate by reading the nuances of waves, sand, snow, moon, and stars. The markers are still there, but most people have lost the ability to see them. Emmi Pikler and Rudolf Steiner were able to read the phenomena of the young child. They used their remarkable capacity to read physical and spiritual realities to offer indications of how to be with children in a way that will offer the greatest possibility for wholeness. As educators and caregivers, we are learning to read the signs, using maps given to us by these two wise teachers to follow the initiative of the child, to honor and respect their wisdom, to create environments that support them, and to work on our own selves to be worthy of them. All this so that they will be as free as possible to wayfind, to find their way.

How each of us finds our way to the work of Dr. Pikler and Dr. Steiner is totally unique to our path and circumstances. This is a beautiful reminder that we are all wayfinding. It is more beautiful still that these wise teachers, and those who take up their indications, continue to work with and for young children so that these developing humans might be as free as possible to choose a path in life, to be who they came here to be, with the least hindrances and the greatest resources. In Waldorf early childhood education, we are so very fortunate that two deeply sensitive, insight-filled streams have "wayfound" each other; that we might be students of the young child and in turn serve the world; and that remarkable women like Debbie, Susan, Jane, and Katherine have found their way to sharing their wisdom with us.

Profound Foundations:
Waldorf Early Childhood Education and the Pikler Approach
Susan Weber

Throughout their lives, Rudolf Steiner, Emmi Pikler, and Pikler's colleagues looked toward a path for growing children such that each could discover and become a unique individual in the world. They offered a foundation of education to optimize this possibility.

I would call this the child's path toward destiny or karma. Steiner and Pikler offered to us, as caregivers and teachers, a path through which we can continue the work of the spiritual beings who enrich and guide the journey of the human being prior to physical birth. In my relationship to Pikler's work, I found this aspect implicit; for Steiner, it is explicit. It is in deep service to the human being that these two streams have found one another, and over time, built bridges for us educators.

Pikler's and Steiner's hope was that educators would develop what we know as a salutogenic approach: Educators would support the development of healthy human beings from the outset, so that the need for remediation would be lessened, if it could not be eliminated. And I believe that each of them in their own way believed that each child is actually a question posed by the spiritual world—a question to which we hope to respond with empathy.

Now, to be clear, Emmi Pikler would perhaps never have articulated this spiritual element. And yet she brought a powerful, unwavering devotion to the freedom of the growing child which speaks to his very essence. I did not sit in intimate conversation with her, although I did have these moments with Anna Tardos, her daughter and my teacher. For both Pikler and Steiner, the child was recognized as a serious being, to be respected and supported. There was no such thing as "sweet" children. Rudolf Steiner articulated a picture of the human being's development over the full span of life. Pikler, similarly, through her capacity for detailed observation of the individual, physical unfolding of the child before her, offered a picture of the very young child's development.

Out of his spiritual research, insights, and experience, Steiner described and articulated a full curriculum and indications for the education of the child beginning at age seven. These indications were carefully recorded by Karl Stockmeyer, one of the very first Waldorf teachers, so that in the future, teachers would have guidance in bringing education to the children in their care.

Pikler and her colleagues similarly offered a path to the care and education of the child in the first three years out of their daily devoted practice and extraordinary archives of film, photo, and care journals. Birth to three was a period that Steiner himself did not articulate for detailed practice as he had with the older child. Pikler offered a roadmap for caregivers and educators of attitudes, gestures, practices. Thus, Pikler made the earthly contributions to complement Steiner's spiritual ones. Perhaps for those of us working in birth to three, Pikler is our Stockmeyer.

This summer, I happened across journalist M. R. O'Connor's *Wayfinding: The Science and Mystery of How Humans Navigate the World* (2019). O'Connor's work intrigued me because it explored a central question of my own: What does it mean to navigate the

The author, wayfinding

world—in the physical realm and also in the higher realms of soul and spirit? How do we develop the capacity to do this?

O'Connor tells the story of getting lost while driving to find a hot spring in New Mexico, because of her reliance upon her GPS. I had a similar experience when traveling to shop at a local garden nursery in Keene. I was not lost, but I encountered a huge sign at the nursery's entrance saying: Turn around here, do NOT follow GPS directions, private property. Curious!

How did O'Connor find her way toward the theme of wayfinding? As with many things in life, it was by getting lost. Being lost despite her GPS awoke a slightly uncomfortable feeling in O'Connor that led to a deeper question about finding one's way.

Like O'Connor and her GPS story, we all have stories where our devices, rather than our senses, lead us. What are some ramifications, and what opportunities lie here? Ultimately, O'Connor's framing research question was this: Can the GPS turn-by-turn function have a subtle and potentially insidious impact on our well-being? Among other encounters, she describes her meeting in Hawaii with Kala Babayan, who learned the traditional means of navigating, by the stars, planets, moon, sun, and the swells of the waves, from some of the last of the indigenous navigators.

Kala sailed alone from Hawaii to Tahiti in a seventy-two-foot canoe—a thirty-day voyage—navigating only by the swells, stars, and wind. What did her experience uncover for her?

"It's completely relying on yourself to see, hear, and feel, there's no modern instruments, there's no compass. It makes me feel good. I'm not lost." Fear, she said, never enters the picture (O'Connor 2019, 246).

She also discovered that her navigation skills felt more akin to spirituality than science. "Some people say traditional navigators were scientists but spirituality was a part of what they did" (O'Connor 2019, 246).

Nainoa Thompson, another navigator, lost his way while journeying in 1980 from Hawaii to Tahiti. Only after getting lost did he glean what he understood to be the mystery of wayfinding in the ocean. One night he lost track of all the directional cues in bad weather and began to panic. He experienced an overwhelming sense of being out of control, of the dread of failure, when suddenly he *felt* the moon above him. Based upon this single sensation, he was convinced he knew where he was and managed to navigate the canoe. "I can't explain it. There was a connection between my senses that went beyond the analytical, beyond seeing with my own eyes. That night, I learned that there are levels of navigation that are realms of the spirit" (O'Connor 2019, 242).

I hope you know where I am headed. What is it that prepares a child to journey in true freedom? Judit Falk, pediatrician and director of Lóczy (the Pikler Institute) for many years, states: "When an adult intervenes in a child's movement and play, not only is there a disturbance of the autonomy of the situation, but the adult's own goals are substituted for the child's interests, and this intervention creates an unnatural dependence upon the adult" (Falk 1994, 44). Just as with the use of a GPS, the adult is substituting their own interests and capacities for the child's.

O'Connor comes to understand that wayfinding is "an activity capable of engaging with and attending to places and nourishing relationships and attachments to them" (O'Conor 2019, 17). Isn't this our very hope as we journey alongside young children as their teachers and caregivers?

The task for both Pikler and Waldorf early childhood educators is to bring security and a sense of self to the child through experience in the world. How does this come about? Through the development of and commitment to a devoted, conscious, empathetic relationship with each child that the adult initiates through consciousness and attention. It is not only through caregiving—not only through the engagement and offering of our gaze and touch. Every opportunity to strengthen this relationship is a golden moment in the infant's and toddler's biography. Steiner describes the life forces in the human eye that reach out with living streams of substance to embrace that which we gaze upon. Our time spent building relationship with the child thus provides reinforcement for human development, expanding from a physical practice to the higher spiritual aspect of the human encounter. It is the foundation for the child's wayfinding.

We commit to offering each child a self-initiated life. Yes, self-initiated bodily movement—rolling, stretching, crawling, walking in one's own time and way. But not only that! Self-initiated play, the child's freedom to choose a path through space, to respond to the daily rhythm in one's individual way and time. As we care for the infant and toddler, each moment is an opportunity to offer autonomy to the child—or to remove it. Moment to moment, the human being connects with destiny and karma, and the echoes of pre-earthly life are carried forward for the individual. We can do tremendous good by carrying a deep awareness in our hearts of the true reality of destiny.

What are our further goals?

- To establish the daily rhythm that supports the construction of the sense of self.

- To cultivate and protect the child's senses. Henning Köhler describes this for us: "Let us remind ourselves that unhurried peacefulness and reverential feeling are the best inner approach and support for everything we do externally in the feeding, warming, bodily care, sleep, and rhythm concerns in the nurturing of the life sense. It allows a child to experience himself as a soul within a body and as a body being energized by a soul" (Köhler 2013).

- To support building the healthiest possible physical body. Rudolf Steiner suggests: "The main task of the teacher or educator is to bring up the body to be as healthy as it possibly can be; this means, to use every spiritual measure to ensure that in later life a human being's body shall give the least possible hindrance to the will of his spirit. If we make this our purpose in school, we can develop the powers which lead to an education for freedom" (Steiner 1922).

These objectives could be considered a description of wayfinding, which in turn could describe the way in which infants and young children learn. The child's capacity to map the physical environment begins early—through the infant's own wayfinding, or self-initiated movement. Each motor movement, even prior to crawling, stimulates the development of the hippocampus, the region of gray matter located in the temporal lobe of the brain that is responsible for two major functions. First, it is responsible for spatial navigation. Second, it takes part in the process of converting short-term to long-term memories. Crucially, it is these memories that enable us to construct our sense of self, a central process for all of life but one that is especially active in the first three years.

When the hippocampus is not adequately stimulated, it will decrease in volume over time. This shrinkage will adversely affect how we solve spatial problems. Researchers confirm that exercising spatial memory and continually finding orientation in daily life will stimulate the growth of the hippocampus, and that underuse in older adults may contribute to cognitive impairment; atrophy in the hippocampus can lead to dementia, depression, PTSD, and Alzheimer's disease.

The hippocampus develops through movement and leads the child into security in the body. During early childhood, the capacity for spatial mapping is especially active as the hippocampus is still developing. Interestingly, the nonmobile infant does not yet form cognitive maps of spatial information, and mainstream researchers feel that without sustained opportunities for children to experience exploratory wayfinding, there will be costs to cognition and memory. Crawling—a major movement threshold—is associated with a significant cognitive leap as self-locomotion prompts hippocampal maturation, ultimately facilitating the creation of the infrastructure for long-term memory (O'Connor 2019, 69).

The unconscious perception of spatial orientation arises from self-generated movements. Therefore, self-initiated activity is critical for the child's development of strong spatial orientation. Self-initiated movement, play, freedom to explore the environment, and freedom to engage the senses are the foundation stones for young children's healthy development. In M. R. O'Connor's work, what we know about the young child's development is explored in a fresh context, through another lens, extending these basic tenets of education and development to the deeper essence of what it means to be human.

As I look at O'Connor's work on wayfinding and recall my own biography, I am confirmed in my conviction that the world is indeed filled with spirit, that the landscape of the earth and the firmament above are life-filled. They demonstrate the living reality of Rudolf Steiner's spiritual science. Being in the world can give us the courage for endless wayfinding on the earth, and in the soul and spiritual realms as well. "[Wayfinding is] an activity [that enables us to become] capable of engaging with and attending to places and nourishing relationships and attachments to them. At a time of social change and ecological disruption, the possibility of this reengagement with our surroundings seems incredibly important" (O'Connor 2019, 17).

As I write this, we have just entered into the season of Michaelmas. Michaelmas offers a mood, an inner experience paramount to our cultivation of the human as a being of heart-filled relationship, of initiative, of will. This time and festival were of great importance to Rudolf Steiner. He offered his final public lecture, in fact, on Michaelmas Eve.

Through the being of Michael we find the strength to see the spiritual in early childhood. In an early lecture, Steiner said:

> It is only during this first period that influences derived from the physical world can be brought to bear upon the physical body in the sense of equipping it with power and strength. And here we find a mysterious connection between the physical body and the consciousness soul. If the Ego is to acquire strength in later life, that is, after the

thirty fifth year, if it is to develop inner activity, penetrating and itself becoming penetrated by the forces of the consciousness soul, so that it can finally transcend itself and acquire knowledge of the world—if this is to be the case the Ego must encounter no boundaries in the physical body for the latter can be the source of the greatest obstacles for the consciousness soul and the Ego, when the Ego would eschew inner seclusion and seek free intercourse with the world (Steiner 1909, 18).

Great strength for all of life's karma arises from the experiences of these earliest years. We hope that through our devoted care, the child will also gain the clarity of mind and awareness of a larger world that will enable him to read the currents of the times with objectivity.

Your empathy for each child on this path, your openness to each generation's possibilities, now arises. The children must be ready to challenge the conventions and the conceptions that no longer apply for our times and must find the courage to bring what is theirs into the coming decades without losing their way.

If each of you as an early childhood educator in the Waldorf/Pikler stream is on a journey of wayfinding, of practicing it, you will sharpen these capacities—not only earthly but also spiritual—in this time of social change and ecological disruption. If you are prepared and alert as wayfinding teachers, you will not only sense what the children in your care need, but will also gain the clarity of mind and the awareness of a larger world that will enable you to read the currents of the times with objectivity.

If you travel the world without a GPS, you will find yourselves on the true journey that will enable you to find your own way and truth, and the light that is yours and yours alone.

The author

REFERENCES

Falk, Judit. 1994. "Forty Years of Lóczy." In *Bulletin of the Sensory Awareness Foundation* 14 (Winter).

Köhler, Henning. 2013. *Difficult Children: There Is No Such Thing*. Chatham, NY: Waldorf Publications.

O'Connor, M. R. 2019. *Wayfinding: The Science and Mystery of How Humans Navigate the World*. New York: St. Martin's Press.

Steiner, Rudolf. 1909. *The Metamorphoses of the Soul*. Forest Row, England: Rudolf Steiner Press.

———. 1922. *The Spiritual Ground of Education*. Lecture 4. The Oxford Course. Hudson, NY: Steiner Books, 2003.

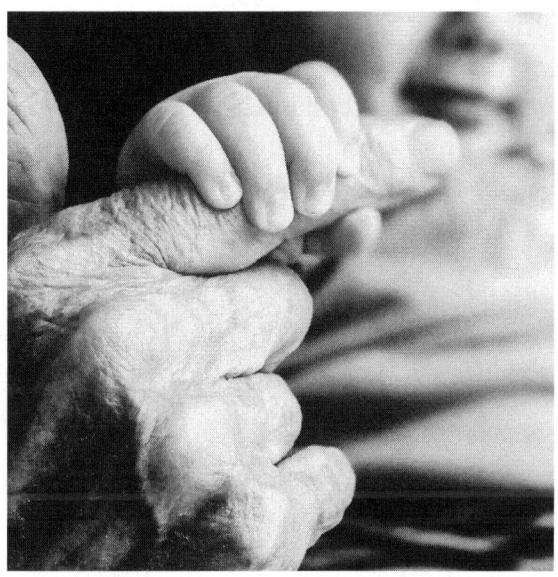

Our Hands, Our Eyes, Our Voices: The Baby's Welcome
Katherine Scharff

During my years working as a nurse, I supported people at the end of their lives. I began to wonder what it was that they really needed from me. I became conscious of what my hands were doing, how my voice sounded, and where my gaze was. I could sense that the overall gesture of my being was felt by the people I cared for, and this was the beginning of my journey to understanding how to truly provide care to another human being. As a caregiver at the end of life, I also made sure the family remained connected with their loved one. Together we created an environment of respect and care, and honored who the loved one had been in life. My experiences with end-of-life care have built the foundation of my work with young children.

When my focus turned to working with young children, it became clear that they were arriving newly from the spiritual world; in attending to those at the end of life, I was preparing them for their spiritual journey into the afterlife. My question as I made this transition became: How will I welcome this new child from the spiritual world to the earth and into the arms of an earthly family?

At birth, infants are born into a foreign world. Everything they experience is new and it can be difficult for them to find their way. They initiate relationships with adults by making it known that they need help, and the adults respond. Very quickly an infant realizes how to communicate with an adult, and as long as the adult responds, the infant continues to communicate needs over and over. Gradually, over time, an infant's capacities grow and develop. It is essential for this growth that the adult learns to observe and listen to the infant in order to build and strengthen this new relationship.

Infants become acquainted with themselves and their physical bodies in the first months of life through their movements and through what they feel, hear, and see. How they are touched, held, and fed shapes this experience and leads the child into the earthly world. To facilitate this process, it is essential for the infant to experience space and opportunity for self-initiated movement, to touch and to see a variety of things, and to hear the voices of those that care for them. Then, in their own time, infants can freely move and explore the world that surrounds them.

When working with a child, an adult facilitates the child's experience through interactions. What kind of mood does the adult create? What are the adult's inner and outer gestures? How are these gestures received by the child? Careful observation makes it clear that children take in what they see and sense in the adults around them. In order to serve the child, it is our task as adults to become aware of ourselves. We begin by sensing what is needed. Is the child ready? Is the child responding with its muscles, movements, eyes? If so, we respond to our observations by providing care. We begin to create a dialogue with the young child, making sure our attention is present and in the moment. Children need us to converse with them, and also need to follow our gestures. We need to gesture slowly, providing pauses to allow the child time to respond.

When creating toddler groups where parents leave children with a caregiver or teacher, an additional gesture is needed. As the children move out further into the space we caregivers hold, they sense it as bigger. Some children will need close connection to an adult and will only wander out as long as they can still sense the etheric being of the caregiver. It may be helpful to give parents who are concerned about their child's well-being a picture of an invisible circle around the child and caregiver as the child finds comfort in a new place. A toddler in one of my preschool classes would remain within such a circle, moving with me about the yard, and when I went too far away from her, she would scream. I had to learn to be aware of her needs, of what she was saying to me, and I had to observe her responses.

Voice and Gesture

Dr. Pikler suggests that every time an adult has an interaction with a child, she has the opportunity to speak to him, to address him, and to let him know that he matters; that she is there for him, that she is present, available, and accepting of him. She observes that the adult's gestures are imperative in creating a dialogue between her and the child (Chahin and Tardos 2017, 61).

A two-year-old child that came to our preschool was pale, did not speak yet, and was unable to walk without falling down every few steps. He did not yet feed himself and would not engage in dressing or undressing. When he fell, he would cry and wanted help getting back up. To begin supporting this child, we observed all of his activities and his responses. We spoke with his parents, who felt they did not know how to support him, and asked them to observe him thoroughly too. After observing all that we could, we were ready to develop a plan to support the child. The plan included such things as slowing down when speaking to and caring for the child, increasing adult presence while caring for the child at home and at school, engaging the child in his daily care needs, and giving opportunities for the child to walk on many different surfaces. Within seven months, he was able to walk, fall, and get back up joyfully, and to eat on his own. He was able to begin dressing himself and to speak in sentences with a few words.

Our hand gestures say a lot about our direct relationships to others. In many cultures, meeting a new person comes with the joining of hands in a handshake. How people gesture with their hands gives a sense of who they are. Our hands are unique in that they can come together from the right and left and meet in the middle. Rudolf Steiner talks about the right and left coming together as bringing self-awareness (Steiner 1989). Western priests demonstrated this when they first brought their hands

together in prayer. In other cultures, it is still a practice to greet another with one's palms brought together. Our hands can be skillful and knowledgeable. When we offer care for the young child we need to be sure our hand gestures are gentle, slow, and tactful. The child must have the opportunity to follow our movements in order to respond with self-initiated activity or will activity. During intimate, caring moments our gestures become the basis of our relationships with children.

The voice can be used to invite participation, dialogue, and relationship in the care of a child. At first the child is hearing the language spoken but may not know what the words mean. To help the child follow what we are saying, our voices need to be rhythmical, slow, and brought with warmth. It is important to speak words to children when leading them into activities. Then they can respond and build their competence with language. It is good to take note that children need to hear their names, not endearing nicknames, as they are differentiating themselves from others. Our names are unique to us and set us apart.

Touch

Safe, gentle touch lowers stress hormones and promotes a sense of safety and security, ultimately changing the brain's wiring and function (Chahin and Tardos 2017, 88, quoting Dr. Natasha Khazonov).

Children learn about the world through our touch as we care for their day-to-day needs. When they experience our hands being attentive, as we help with handwashing or nose-wiping for example, they learn about the world. Additionally, children develop relationships with adults through these moments of care. Developing children become more and more competent in their own care, but there will still be moments that they need adult help and will wish for connection with an adult. As the child becomes more competent in self-care, the adult can turn toward observing and waiting to see where and when the child needs attention. As the caregiver, your hands can rest on your lap or at your sides, but can remain in a gesture of being ready to help if needed, a gesture of anticipation, or of guiding. Confusion comes for young children when our hands and our words are not congruent. When our hands hurry to get a child's coat on after we have just communicated slowly that it is time to go outside, the child experiences a confusing moment.

A very important part of our work is the use of touch games. These lead the child into an experience of physical touch as well as a sense of being bathed in language. Wilma Ellersiek calls the touch games "caresses." They support children's experiences of their bodies as they become acquainted with themselves. A two-year-old girl in my preschool often screams and runs around the classroom, but can stop herself and ask for a touching game on her face which helps her to calm and recenter. One day the child told her mother to sit down when she felt her mother was anxious, and slowly touched her mother's face as she said the verse.

Our Hands, Our Eyes, Our Voices: The Baby's Welcome

Our Eyes and Gaze

The eyes
These lovely lamps, whose sweet sparks lively turning
These windows of the soul, these starry twins
(Du Bartas 1611, 158)

Our eyes and gaze become one in the relationship with the child. Children see adults and respond not only with their eyes but with their whole bodies as they move in response to the moment of connection. If you meet an older child, it is important to carefully observe what the child needs rather than questioning directly, with a direct gaze. Looking directly into the child's eyes might be too much; the child would often be better supported by a soft gaze. We often ask children to speak to and look at a new person when they meet them. The child may not be ready for this, and it is up to the adult to assess what the child needs at that moment. There was a child I had in my class who hid behind her mother each time they approached the play yard. She would peek from behind her mother's legs to see me. If I looked at her, she would hide again but if I looked at and engaged with her mother, the child would make her way into the yard, usually giving me a quick hug and then going off to play. It took many months before I could even look at her with a soft gaze.

∽

By immersing himself in the process of forming sounds as it takes place, and in making the word-gesture together with the adult, the child comes to know and live within the form through which the language arises (Ellersiek 2003, 15).

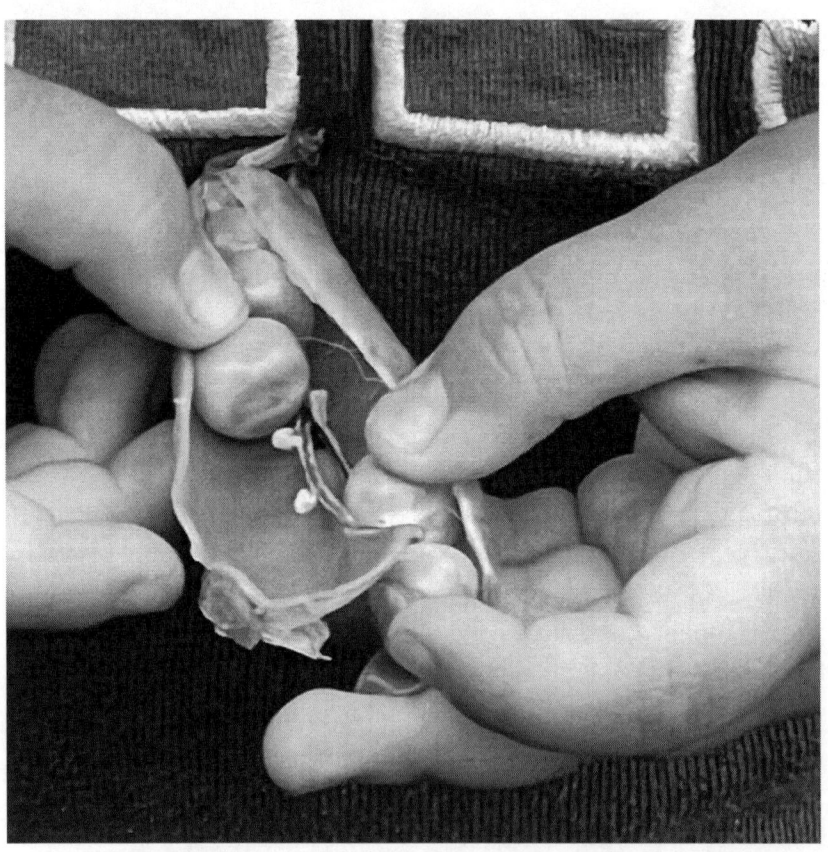

One works with gestures, hands, eyes, and voice in creating a dialogue with children. We learn from them when we find harmony in the relationship, just as they learn from us. In doing so, we support the young child in becoming human.

REFERENCES

Chahin, Elsa, and Anna Tardos. 2017. *In Loving Hands: How the Rights for Young Children Living in Children's Homes Offer Hope and Happiness in Today's World*. N.p: by the authors.

Du Bartas, Guillaume de Salluste. 1611. *Du Bartas His Deuine Weekes and Workes Translated: and Dedicated to the Kings Most Excellent Maiestie by Iosuah Syluester*. The Sixt Daie of the First Week. Early English Books Online Text Creation Partnership (EEBOTCP). Accessed April 21, 2022. http://name.umdl.umich.edu/A11395.0001.001.

Ellersiek, Wilma. 2003. *Giving Love, Bringing Joy*. Lyn and Kundry Wilwerth, transl. Spring Valley, NY: Waldorf Early Childhood Association of North America.

Steiner Rudolf. 1989. Lecture to the Workman, Dec. 13, 1922. In *The Human Being in Body, Soul, and Spirit: Our Relationship to the Earth*. Hudson, NY: Anthroposophic Press.

Understanding and Supporting Free Movement from Birth to Three
Jane Swain

This chapter describes the author's professional and personal insights based on her study at the Pikler Institute, her study of Spacial Dynamics®, her pediatric physical therapy training, and her observations of children and families in her care.

For some time, it has been the norm in our culture for adults to routinely place infants in activity saucers, infant seats, swings, and other types of baby equipment, sometimes for extended periods of their days.

I am a pediatric physical therapist. Members of my profession have long advocated against the use of baby equipment that places an infant in sitting or standing positions before the baby can manage the position with any degree of ease or control. Simply stated, when babies are placed in such equipment, they are not free to move in the natural ways that babies move. This restriction of large motor movements works against the development of coordinated movement. These babies are missing out on important motor learning that occurs in the foundational stages, before sitting or standing, and in the experience of moving into and out of sitting and standing positions.

A Science-Based Alternative to Baby Equipment

In addition to training as a physical therapist, I have studied the work of Rudolf Steiner and Emmi Pikler, who, rather than speaking out so much against the use of baby equipment, spoke out in favor of its polar opposite, supporting freely initiated movement. Out of a profound depth and breadth of spiritual scientific knowledge of the human being, Steiner gave general indications for the care of infants and toddlers. Pikler performed well-documented, observational research with the infants and young children in her care over a seventeen-year period. Out of this work, she developed a detailed approach to caring for the young child.

Steiner and Pikler didn't know each other and they came from very different vantage points, yet they were remarkably similar in their fundamental belief that no one knew better than the infants themselves how best to move and how best to learn to move. Both Steiner and Pikler advocated that the infant be allowed the freedom to negotiate their own motor journey up into verticality at their own pace, in their own individualized way, without overt instruction and without encouragement from an adult. They trusted the infant's innate ability to learn to roll over by themselves, to know whether to spend a longer or shorter time belly crawling, and ultimately how quickly or slowly to progress up into standing and walking.

There is no need to teach a typical infant to move in new ways that they have not yet attempted, nor to place them into positions that they cannot yet get into or out of on their own. Instead, Steiner and Pikler advocated freedom of movement (within safe boundaries) for the child. In this approach, the adult holds a deep appreciation for what the child is doing out of their own initiative, and doesn't expect, help, or encourage them do what they are not yet capable of doing. The adult creates an appropriate space in which the child can do their own work, knowing that it is theirs to do.

Observation: A Key to Supporting the Baby's Self-Learning

This self-initiated approach to motor learning is unfamiliar to most adults in our culture, and it may even go against the instincts of some. To many adults, it is not readily apparent that an infant is actively working on a plethora of skills while in a horizontal position, and so the adult may respond by helping the child come up into verticality. It has been my experience that adults are more likely to support a child-led approach to motor learning if they learn to observe what the child is working on and accomplishing over time, especially in the early positions of back-lying (lying supine), side-lying, and tummy-lying (lying prone). It is largely unrecognized that the back-lying infant is working to develop head control. In a brand-new baby, the head extends and rolls to either side; the newborn and very young infant literally can't align their head along the centrally located midline (which separates the right side of the body from the left), due to the influences of the primitive reflexes. Indeed, the first manifestation of head control occurs in back-lying, as the baby learns to tuck their chin, bring their head to midline, and then keep it there for longer and longer periods of time. This development of head control gives the baby's eyes a stable base from which to work and is foundational for eye tracking and convergence.

The baby also does a lot of other things while back-lying, like looking at the hands, turning and moving the hands closer and farther away from the eyes (another huge milestone in eye-hand coordination), playing with toys, putting hands and toys in the mouth, bringing hands to the right/left midline, pulling at clothes, touching hands to one knee and then to both knees simultaneously, and touching hands to one foot and then to both feet simultaneously.

Some infants will spend many months lying on their backs, learning to hold toys between their feet and pass toys from their feet

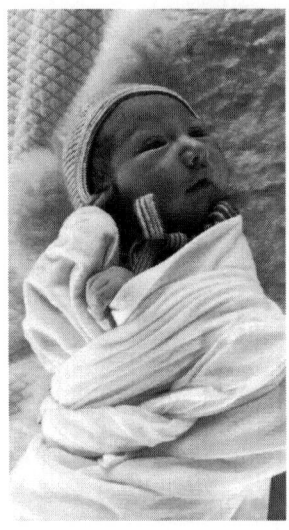 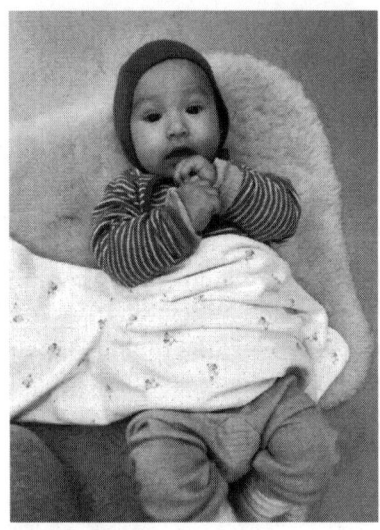

Left: The typical newborn posture, with head extended and rotated to the side. Right: The same child several months later. Note that he is now able to align his head, hands, and eyes along the right/left midline of his body.
Photos courtesy of Morgan Heringer

to their hands. Sometimes they hold a toy with their hands and another toy with their feet and bang the two together. This activity has all the mastery of a jazz musician's improvisation, and it is an amazingly artistic activity to witness, if one is so lucky. The child is showing themselves to us through the activities they are drawn to, and we come to know them in deeper ways. Perhaps this child will grow up and become a juggler in a circus, or is preparing to juggle many aspects of a rich and busy life. We may marvel at the focus and tenacity required to explore such a complex task. The quiet joy that the baby exudes during such self-initiated activity is noteworthy.

If our observations of the child have a heart-warmed quality, they can serve as the foundation of an invisible, rich ethos surrounding and supporting the child. Children are very sensitive to the way they are observed. Thus, with curiosity, genuine interest, and openness for what the child may reveal to us, we can recognize the majestic role self-initiated motor development plays in the expression of the child's individuality.

Parents may also come to a self-initiated movement approach by learning to observe their child's developing balance. When asked what positions require balance, most people relate balance to standing. This makes sense. Most people have suffered a fall when walking. Most have not fallen when they were sitting or lying on their backs, for example. However, in the infant, balance develops and exists in every developmental position, and also during the transitions between positions.

Hence, balance is explored and fine-tuned within the positions of back-lying, side-lying, tummy-lying, on hands and knees, sitting, kneeling, squatting, and standing. Balance is also cultivated when the baby transitions between two positions, such as from back-lying to side-lying, from sitting to hands and knees,

This child is new to tummy-lying. Her balance has not yet developed much in this position, as seen by the low center of mass. *Photo courtesy of Cynthia D. Cote*

This child is more experienced in tummy-lying. She has developed more balance in the position, as seen by the higher center of mass. *Photo courtesy of Cynthia D. Cote*

This child is very new to side-lying. Her balance has not yet developed much in this position, as seen by the wide base of support. *Photo courtesy of Benjamin Swain*

Understanding and Supporting Free Movement from Birth to Three

This is the same child (from bottom of page 42) at a later point when she is more experienced in side-lying. She has developed more balance in the position, as seen by the narrower base of support. *Photo courtesy of Benjamin Swain*

or from squat to stand. Within and between positions, we can observe objective changes over time in the width of the child's base of support and in the height of their center of mass. As balance develops, the width of the base of support narrows, and the height of the center of mass increases.

A Nuanced Progression of Balance

In each developmental position, there is a progression of balance. The infant learns to achieve a new developmental position and then learns to maintain the position over longer periods of time. Maintaining the position can be more difficult than one would think, because it requires a finely tuned interplay of muscles. As infants explore being in a position, they move a little bit—perhaps by waving their arms, reaching, or turning their heads—and with these subtle movements, their center of mass shifts. The infant's body—especially their core—then has to accommodate the weight shift, or else they may fall out of the position. Learning to balance includes losing one's balance, and our bodies go through all manner of gyrations when we lose our balance, with the primary purpose of preventing our heads from hitting the ground. Sometimes we lose our balance, but recover it shortly after we start to fall, and so we don't actually hit the floor. Babies do this frequently as they move through each of the gross motor positions.

There is incredible wisdom at play when the child is given the time and space to negotiate the motor sequence at their own direction. In this scenario, the child takes the next step only after sufficient preparation, and only the child knows when this is. For example, losing and recovering balance and learning how to fall in the lower positions of back-lying, side-lying, and tummy-lying—where there is less height from which to fall—is valuable preparation for when the baby gets to the higher positions of kneeling and standing—where potential falls are from greater heights. If a baby has had opportunities to develop nuanced balance reactions in the lower positions, they are less likely to have head injuries when they reach standing and early walking.

We can recognize when an infant has recently achieved a developmental position, because they characteristically use a wide base of support in it. As their balance develops in that position, we can recognize this too, because the base of support typically narrows. After a while, the child's balance in the new position may be good enough to let them manage playing with toys. Playing with toys makes keeping balance in the new position a more complex task, because it typically involves still more shifting of weight within the position. With resultant postural adjustment, the base of support may widen again. As the child gains more competency with balance when playing with toys, the base of support again narrows.

Development doesn't proceed at a predictable rate. It slows down, bursts forward, meanders, and returns again and again to what the adult may interpret as a previous stage. For example, even if a child is crawling and pulling up to stand, they may return to playing on their back. In fact, even two-year-olds will occasionally lie on their backs, hold a dolly up on their shins, and play in that position. When youngsters have opportunities to freely chose the positions in which they play, it can be very comforting to go back to "home base" and play there from time to time. This is one way the child learns to self-regulate.

Supporting Motor Learning in the Transitions

Balance develops in nuanced but observable ways in each developmental position. It also develops in the transitions between positions. Therefore, it is helpful to employ practices that encourage the baby to engage in transitional movements. The following practice is applicable for a baby who has not yet achieved the verticality of sitting, and is still primarily playing in the horizontal positions of back-lying, side-lying, and tummy-lying. After changing or feeding the baby, one can return them to the play area by placing them on their back. This can be done even if the baby will immediately transition to tummy-lying. Again, it is helpful if the baby has many opportunities to transition, because they are refining balance during each transition.

It is also helpful to pick up a baby from the back-lying position at this stage of development. If the infant is playing on their tummy, the caregiver can approach the child and orient them by saying, "I'm going to turn you over onto your back, and then pick you up." Gradually the child will turn onto their back on their own when the adult comes to pick them up. Learning this practice can be empowering for the infant, because it gives them a concrete way to cue the adult that they want to be picked up. My grandchild, when she was at this stage, would belly crawl over to one of her parents, turn onto her back, wave her arms, and kick her legs, signaling, "Please pick me up!" One time during supper, she belly crawled near to her mother and performed this maneuver. Her mother replied, "I'm going to finish my plate, and then I'll pick you up," and she kept eating. My granddaughter promptly belly crawled closer—through the legs of her mother's chair—and turned over, so that she was directly in front of her mother. She waved her arms and kicked her legs more emphatically, indicating, "Please pick me up now!", and her mother did.

Far-Reaching Effects of the Adult's Gesture toward the Child

The adult's gesture of valuing and supporting the child's active and unique explorations of their world and their movements can have far-reaching effects. Through this approach, the children are given opportunities to achieve highly refined, well-earned balance and motor capacities, and much more. Because they themselves have done the work without taking any shortcuts, they can authentically have the credit for it. This process lends itself to the child's development of a deeply held, quiet confidence in themselves. This process also supports the child's total engagement. They give it their all! As a result, they come into a self-directed rhythm of getting good and tired out, then stopping to rest. Or perhaps they become frustrated with the task they have chosen and want a break from it. They may come back to it later, or not. They learn to pace themselves naturally because they are not bound by outside encouragement. No one is urging them to continue when they've had enough. This is an important stage for the development of self-regulation.

A freely initiated approach to movement for infants and toddlers can have wide-ranging benefits for the adults as well. We say in the United States that one has "found oneself." We say this when we have a particular relationship with our deeds: We are highly interested, deeply satisfied and nourished, and fully engaged. Through freely initiated movement opportunities, infants and toddlers have opportunities to find themselves by recognizing and exploring their own interests and ways of doing. We adults witness the child's small but mighty acts of creation as they bravely venture forth, coming into their bodies and out into the world, learning to successfully meet the world through their play and movements. If supported, the child's acts of creation increase in number and evolve over time. What are they creating? They are creating themselves. Many wise experts have discovered that to feel seen is to feel loved. As we adults support and witness the free movements and creations of our infants and youngsters, we are afforded a unique way of knowing and seeing them, because we may catch glimpses of who they—in freedom—truly are becoming.

Birth to Three in Education and Care

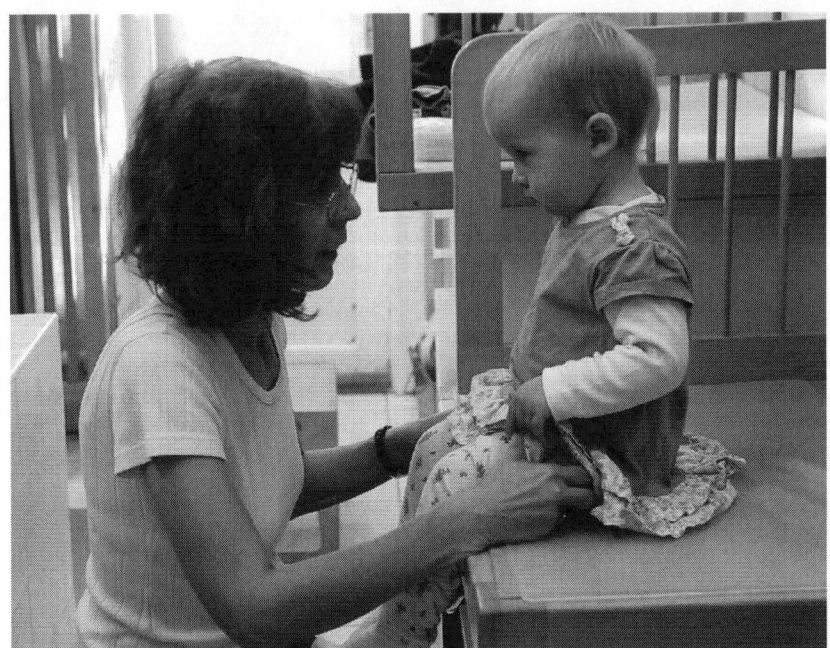

The photos above illustrate the free movement of the child in the dressing and diapering routines and the shared interest that lives between the caregiver and the child in the experience.

Caregiver Interactions with Infants and Toddlers During Diapering:
Caregiver Responsiveness, Child Well-being, and Involvement
Deborah Laurin, PhD

I owe my gratitude to Dr. Emmi Pikler (1902–1984), who first dared to think differently about children, and to all the caregivers and many colleagues at the Emmi Pikler House, where the adults allow young children enough time to be children. Rarely had I observed caregiver responses and an attitude based on the premise that children "from infancy, are active, proactive, and autonomous at their own level—and a partner for adults" (Szántó-Feder 2020).

Dr. Emmi Pikler, pediatrician, orthopedist, scientist, and visionary, documented in scientific and anecdotal detail the experiences of the children and caregivers in Budapest, Hungary, at a children's residential nursery. Now a childcare center, the Emmi Pikler House continues with a unique approach, still ahead of its time and independent of the status quo, where the caregiver-child relationship is expressed as a meeting of two free people. The caregiver has a leading role, yet gives the child space, so that the child is a participant in the care experience with the adult.

Approached from this perspective, diapering becomes a shared process where the child is actively involved and the caregiver's attitude and actions matter. Is the caregiver, with sensitivity, able to read and interpret the social, emotional, and motor cues of the child? Will the caregiver put aside any sense of urgency and alter their tempo to allow the child time to absorb the experience and adjust for what comes next?

I returned from Budapest with many questions that became the catalyst for the seeds of my US diaper study. I began to explore diapering care in the cultural context of a US midwestern city, as opposed to the context of the Pikler House in Hungary, to re-envision diapering practices and ignite discussion about the significance of this routine in the caregiver–infant and toddler relationship, especially in group care where children frequently experience multiple caregivers and, at times, and a one-size-fits-all, custodial approach to diapering. We observed the caregiver's direct responsiveness and the impact of the adult's interactions on the child's well-being and involvement. I hypothesized that the quality of caregiver interactions during diapering would relate to children's experiences, especially in the social-emotional realm.

This correlational study in a US midwestern city involved 31 caregivers, with 74 infants and toddlers in 30 infant and toddler classrooms and 144 separate diapering changes. Based on these observations, we concluded:

> Caregiver responsiveness was found to be significantly related to both child involvement and child well-being. Another feature of caregivers' behavior, caregiver encouragement, was significantly associated with child well-being, but not child involvement. The study results suggest that caregivers' behaviors, specifically responsiveness and encouragement, during diapering are vital in the moment-to-moment interactions between a caregiver

and child. Responsiveness and encouragement in care routines should be emphasized in infant care settings and should be a focus for caregiver professional development, including pre- and in-service training. While training related to diapering is often restricted to health concerns, the findings suggest that specific caregiver-child interactions during this care routine may support or hinder children's well-being and involvement in the moment. Caregiver responsiveness to children's cues in this context may enhance children's opportunities to practice involvement with the caregiver and thus, support children's well-being (Laurin, Guss, & Horm 2021, 546).

More Than Efficiency

Do you remember the first time you changed a diaper? It may have been an awkward, tense, and even fearful experience. With practice, perhaps you became efficient. But diapering is about more than gaining efficiency. When approached with an attitude of appreciation for the infant, when the experiences of the child resonate within you and guide your actions on the child's behalf, diaper-changing becomes a care routine transformed from hygienic efficiency to working with the child's wholeness and well-being.

A sizable portion of an infant's and toddler's day involves bodily care routines—over five thousand diaper changes in the first three years (Gerber 2000). Frequently approached with haste, on average three minutes in length, diaper-changing and other toileting routines are typically not appreciated as a central element in infant and toddler classroom care (Laurin 2019). With efficiency in mind, disease prevention and hygienic procedures shape most caregiver interactions. By contrast, Pikler-style care routines are an important ritual for supporting the wholeness of the heart, as a circle of security to the child themselves, a safe sphere where the child experiences the caregiver's warmth and responsiveness, which directly affect the child's rhythmical system. Thus, the heart and rhythmical system are regulated through the child-caregiver relationship. Caregivers can reflect: Where am I putting my attention? Am I paying attention to the mechanics of doing?

Sensorimotor Impressions

"Encounters between children and caregivers are characterized by the joy of the time spent together. And each of them does their best to contribute to that in their own way" (Szántó-Feder 2020, 57). When diapering is associated with pleasant, spontaneous movement, the child is likely to form positive sensorimotor impressions, especially when caregiver responses are attuned to the child's motor activity. Is the caregiver able to follow the child's pauses and rests? For example, by averting the gaze and turning the head away, the child can prompt a positive or negative change in caregiver response. Will the caregiver demonstrate motoric empathy and follow the child's other interests when the child playfully departs from the caregiver's request? Will the caregiver respond with positivity to the child's spontaneous rhythms and WILL movement (McMillan 2017)? This requires the caregiver's internal flexibility, because they will have to temporarily diverge from the task at hand—diapering and dressing the child—and set aside the need for "inconsiderate rushing" (Szántó-Feder 2020, xxiii). For example, a caregiver in a diapering routine might follow the child's interest and playfulness beyond the purpose of the activity. A caregiver would respond to the child's delight and interest in their environment while at the same time guiding the child through the process of diapering.

Children absorb sensory information at a different pace than adults, so slowing down and paying attention to the child's signals becomes vital to how a child begins to feel about their body and bodily functions. Think of the powerful forces of water

Caregiver Interactions with Infants and Toddlers During Diapering

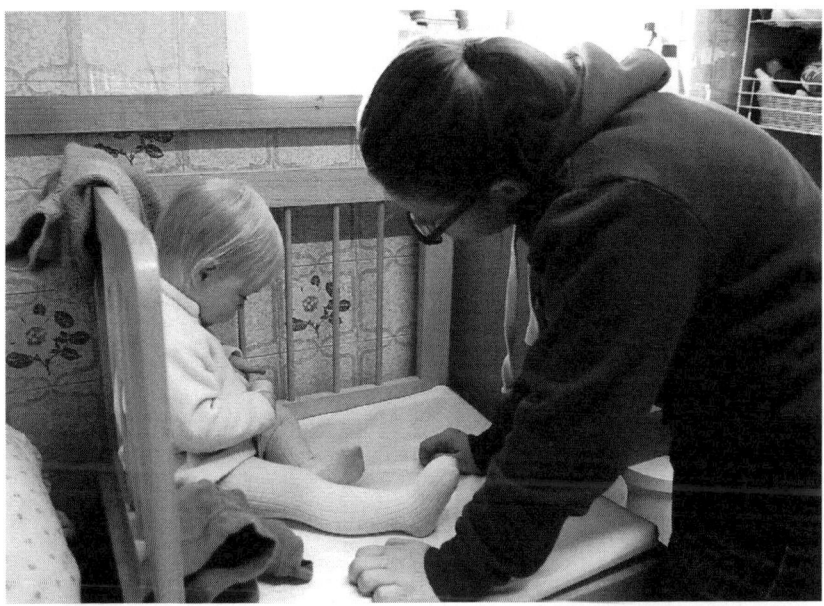

The photos above illustrate the free movement of the child in the dressing and diapering routines and the shared interest that lives between the caregiver and the child in the experience.

shaping rocks, of the dynamic etheric of these elements: One forms the other and the other forms back. Jaimen McMillan stated, "Rhythm trains the WILL and replaces FORCE" (McMillan 2017). How do children express their WILL, and movement created with their WILL, through motor movement? How does the adult call it into life? In the limb activity, the soul force of the child's developing WILL is visible. The child's intelligence and WILL are visible through their expressive body movements. Through movement created with their WILL, the child's experience is having an impact on the experience of the caregiver to sustain a companionable relationship as one forms the other and other forms back.

To help us understand the child's sensorimotor-affective experience, we can be curious and interested and ask ourselves: What is the child's internal state of being? It is helpful to explore the following two vignettes contrasting caregiver-toddler diaper changes to sense into the child's well-being. When we imagine the child's experience by considering the child's cues, what do we conclude the child want us to know? Do the caregivers respond with motoric empathy and a feeling for the child's sensorimotor affective experience?

The following vignettes are from the author's personal observations.

Maia at Thirty Months, 2017

> Placed on the diaper-changing table without warning or comment from her caregiver, Maia, age thirty months, is swiftly picked up from behind, her play abruptly disrupted. Talking to her colleague, the caregiver pulls Maia's pants down, quickly removes her diaper, smiles briefly, and begins to wipe Maia's bottom without talking to the child. Maia's tension and discomfort are clear as

she attempts to turn her body away from her caregiver. Unable to move her body, Maia turns her head away and grabs the raised edge of the changing table with her fingers. She is crying, but her caregiver continues diapering with no acknowledgement of Maia's distress or her tears. With swift, forceful movements, the caregiver applies cream to Maia's vulva. Maia's legs are outstretched and stiff with tension as she protests with cries. Continuing without eye contact or communication, the caregiver puts a clean diaper on Maia, lifts her to standing, pulls her pants up, and lifts her from the change table with a perfunctory comment: "All done." The caregiver washes her hands, but not Maia's. The diaper change is finished in less than one minute.

This vignette evokes a powerful image of a child's distress and a caregiver's focus on the custodial elements of diapering. When repeatedly associated with negative representations, caregiver intrusiveness, and inconsistent practices, a child may respond with passiveness, disassociating from the process, or with behaviors fraught with tension, distress, and resistance. In this vignette we experience the caregiver's force and intrusive, mechanical touch where Maia's sensorimotor movements and affective state reflects the child's internal state in response to her diapering experience. If this becomes the repeated pattern with Maia, what sensorimotor impressions may she come to associate with diaper-changing?

I was visibly shaken and experienced a powerful epiphany after witnessing this diaper change. When do the seeds of consent take shape? From infancy, when we become aware of what we do with children. At the center of young children's learning are their bodies, using sensory, somatic, tactile, and movement experiences to send powerful messages to the brain and rhythmical system, signaling how a child learns about themselves and their environment (Laurin & Goble 2018; Tardos 2016). Sensitive care is associated with higher levels of child well-being and lower levels of cortisol (stress hormone), compared with less sensitive caregiving practices. How has the child integrated sensorimotor affective impressions during the bodily care routines? This is significant. In the nonverbal development of the infant, key sensory impressions or implicit bodily memories are being formed. The affective quality of the caregiver in voice intonation, gestures, attitude, facial expression, and tempo influences how a child interprets the caring moment.

Being cared for is the infant's first experience. The child learns what it is to be cared for and, by extension, eventually expands this experience to the capacity to care for and about others. It follows that we want to work on ourselves by striving to become aware of a child's motivation and volition with us in the relationship, to ensure that the child's etheric body remains anchored in the child, and that sensorimotor affective impressions are not disturbing or jarring. Filtered through the adult's caring, protective presence, the infant's experience of "who I am with" surpasses all else in the nurturing care of the moment. Dr. Johanna Steegmans stated that "In spite of what is around, [caregivers] give the child the sense that 'I see you, I love you, I accept you the way you are' … What flows between the caregiver and child in this way will counteract what is in the environment, even the effects of war" (Steegmans and Karnow 2012, 100).

The following observation at the Pikler Institute in Budapest, Hungary demonstrates a caregiver's approach to the diapering routine where the child, at twenty-eight months, moves with intention and anticipation, happily cooperating and participating in her diapering care.

Villő at Twenty-Eight Months, 2014

Villő is competently involved in the diapering routine with Gabi, her caregiver. Moments before, Villő nimbly stepped up on the little stool in front of the dressing table, then easily pulled herself to standing on the table by holding on to the child-height rails that surround two sides of the table. With synchronous actions, Villő and Gabi engage in the diapering routine with care, respect, and cooperation, at a tempo that allows time for Villő to participate. Once able to stand on their own, the Pikler children frequently participate in diapering from a vertical position as observed in this vignette.

> Gabi begins to unzip Villő's pants, speaking softly, in a conversational style, as she helps to push Villő's pants over the challenging bulk of her diaper. Pausing, Gabi waits while Villő, standing, pushes her pants the remainder of the way to her ankles. Now, Villő seats herself for better stability, because pushing the pants over her foot presents a greater challenge. Gabi knowingly assists. Easing the pant leg over Villő's foot, Gabi stops at her toes. Gabi does not complete the task for the toddler. Instead, she waits for Villő to finish the task, first pulling one pant leg over her toes and then the other. How satisfied Villő looks as she shares a mutual smile with Gabi!

This second vignette reveals Villő's interest, will, and competency to participate in her diapering care. With a light touch, quiet dialogue, and knowing gestures, Gabi responds and pauses as Villő completes her task. It's crucial to note Gabi's sensitivity to pace, timing, and the sequence of undressing. This is an example of a successful choreography because of authentic cooperation and mutual tuning in. For example, Gabi pauses when Villő makes bodily adjustments and sits down on the dressing table to remove her pants. Gabi approaches with empathy for Villő's movement. Note that the caregiver does not move the child into position.

Significantly, the vignette exemplifies learning appropriate to a young child's abilities, as the caregiver supports the scaffolding of complexities into small, concrete tasks. Villő pushes her pants down, then pulls the pants over her toes. Each sequence of this caregiver-child dance depends on the caregiver's sensitive awareness of the subtleties in gesture, communication, timing, and touch. Thus, an internalized pattern of expectancy, of sculpting forces, formed through rhythm, routine, and access to free movement, reveals itself in Villő's and Gabi's external anticipatory responses. Gabi as the primary caregiver knows diapering details unique to Villő. Thus, they act together in the true sense of a partnership. Gabi's pedagogical decisions, guided by the child's volition and motivation, as expressed through Villő's motor movement in the routine, support Villő's zone of proximal development (ZPD) and her WILL development.

For instance, in the vignette, Villő, unrestricted by her caregiver, is free to move on the surface of the changing table, significantly influencing her ability to participate with Gabi in her diapering care. Notably, by standing, Villő interacts on the same plane as Gabi, inferring a more equitable approach to the diapering relationship. Alternately, diapering in the supine position would impinge Villő's ability to act with spontaneity and to express the unique characteristics of her toddler personality that are revealed in the following account.

> Now washing is complete. Villő, standing, removes a wipe from the package and cleans her vulva, then places the wipe in the garbage bag Gabi is holding ready. Gabi takes another wipe and, gesturing, she speaks to Villő, who in response cooperatively lifts her leg to assist Gabi in the washing task. Standing, Villő gazes through a window

at the children playing in the other room. Gabi follows Villő's gaze. Noticing the toddler's interest in the children's play, Gabi pauses in the diapering process to narrate the activity that has captured Villő's attention. When Villő's attention shifts back to the diapering, Gabi offers two diapers for Villő to choose from. Gabi holds them up, and in a moment of playfulness, Villő chooses with her toes. They both smile at this. Their eyes meet before Villő turns to hold the rail with both hands, her legs apart in a wider stance, as Gabi places the diaper, secures the tabs, then snaps the onesie closed.

Ezster Mozes (2016) explained how the caregiver, while observing, may briefly suspend activity. For example, Gabi followed Villő's gaze and interest, pausing in the diapering care to listen and talk to Villő in a moment of shared mental states or joint attention. Villő's playfulness in selecting between two diapers with her toes highlights a joyful diapering experience, where in novel ways, spontaneity is welcome. Importantly, the diapering scenario shines a light on the anchored moment between Gabi and Villő. With a wider stance for stability, Villő's bodily adjustment facilitates placing and securing the new diaper. Villő thus aids Gabi's task. Interweaving elements of care and learning in the concrete moments guided by the child's cues, Gabi does not restrict Villő's movement, interests, or participation. Thus, the high number of moment-to-moment interactions occurring between Gabi and Villő in the diapering environment likely contributes to the toddler's competence and growing sense of self. We can imagine the existence of a "third space" that allows the caregiver vital time for the child to absorb what has happened and adjust for what comes next. For example, pausing with an open gesture of our hands conveys a message of invitation. The simple gesture of touching the child's buttons or sleeve gives a moment for the child to make a bodily adjust and to prepare—to anticipate what comes next.

Diaper-changing is a key opportunity for a child to have an inner experience of what it is to be cared for. What meaning does a child extract from the diapering relationship when touched with haste, treated as an object, and without sensitive, reciprocal exchanges by a caregiver? In care theory, it is through the day-to-day experiences of being cared for that the capacity to care for others is learned. Is this where the seeds of empathy and consent begin? Ensuring that infants and toddlers flourish and thrive in classrooms for their age group requires that care routines be re-envisioned and approached as significant one-on-one experiences, for conveying reverence for the dignity of the child in our actions as deeds, through our head, heart, and hands.

Adopting an approach to diaper-changing based on collaborative care—caring *with*—invites us to broaden the scope of infant and toddler pedagogy to include diaper change routines and all care routines as vital elements of the moment-to-moment caregiver–infant and toddler interactions. It offers infinite possibilities, unique each time, for undiscovered moments of new potential to emerge in the care relationship between a caregiver and child to support the wholeness and well-being of the child.

> *Editor's note: The beautiful images in this chapter have been shared by the Pikler House. We are grateful for the permission granted from the Pikler House to use the images in this publication.*

REFERENCES

Gerber, M. 2000. *The RIE Manual: For Parents and Professionals*. Los Angeles: Resources for Infant Educarers.

Laurin, D. 2019. "One Diaper at a Time: Re-Envisioning Diapering Routines with Infants and Toddlers." *ZERO TO THREE* (Nov.): 11–19.

Laurin, D., & C. Goble. 2018. "Enhancing the Diapering Routine: Caring, Communication, and Development." *Young Children* 73, no. 3: 18–25.

Laurin, D. E., S. S. Guss, & D. Horm. 2021. "Caregiver–Infant and Toddler Interactions During Diapering: Caregiver Responsiveness and Child Well-being and Involvement." *Infant Mental Health Journal* 42, no. 4: 546–559 (July/August).

McMillan, Jaimen. 2017. Spatial Dynamics. Workshop presented at the École Rudolf Steiner de Montréal, November 24, 2017.

Mozes, E. 2016. "Nonviolent Early Care and Education Based on the Pikler Approach." Workshop at the Pikler Summer Intensive. Lóczy, Budapest, Hungary.

Steegmans, Johanna, and Gerald Karnow. 2012. *Cradle of a Healthy Life: Early Childhood and the Whole of Life*. Spring Valley, NY: Waldorf Early Childhood Association of North America.

Szántó-Feder, A. 2020. *Moving with Pleasure from the Beginning*. N.p.: published by the author.

Tardos, A. 2016. "Nonviolent Early Care and Education Based on the Pikler Approach." Workshop at the Pikler Summer Intensive. Lóczy, Budapest, Hungary.

Vincze, M. 1994. "The Meaning of Cooperation During Care Dressing on the Diapering Table, Dressing Table, Cushion." In *Bringing Up and Providing Care for Infants and Toddlers in an Institution*, edited by A. Tardos. Budapest: Pikler-Lóczy Tarsasag.

Recommended Resources

Chahin, Elsa and Anna Tardos. *In Loving Hands: How the Rights for Young Children Living in Children's Homes Offer Hope and Happiness in Today's World*. N.p.: published by the authors, 2017.

Dögl, Pia, Elke Maria Rischke, and Ute Strub. *Beginning Well: Care for the Child from Birth to Age Three*. Spring Valley, NY: Waldorf Early Childhood Association of North America, 2018.

Falk, Judit, and Maria Vincze. *Bathing the Baby: The Art of Care*. Translated by Alex Kajtár. Budapest: Pikler-Lóczy Társaság, 2006.

Glöckler, Michaela and Claudia Grah-Wittich. *The Dignity of the Young Child: How Can We Keep the Young Child Healthy? Care and Up-Bringing in the First Three Years of Life*. Dornach: Rudolf Steiner Press, 2021.

Heckmann, Helle. *Slow Parenting: Caring for Children with Intention*. Phoenixville, PA: Lilipoh Publishing, Inc., 2011.

———. *Nøkken: A Garden for Children*. Second edition. Spring Valley, NY: Waldorf Early Childhood Association of North America, 2016.

———. *Five Golden Keys: Towards an Embracing Developing Life with Small Children Under Seven Years of Age*. N.p.: Slowparenting.dk, 2017.

———. *Loving Care for the Child Under Three: Handbook for Caregivers, Insight for Parents*. N.p.: Slow Parenting, 2021.

Johnson, Stephanie. *Baby Bare: A Bottom-Up Approach to Growing Strong Brains and Bodies*. Minneapolis: Wiselnk Creative Publishing, 2016.

Kálló, Éva and Györgyi Balog. *The Origins of Free Play*. Budapest: The Pikler Institute, 1996.

Patzlaff, Rainer, Claudia McKeen, Ina von Mackensen, and Claudia Grah-Wittich. *The Child from Birth to Three in Waldorf Education and Child Care*. Second edition. Spring Valley, NY: Waldorf Early Childhood Association of North America, 2020.

Raichle, Bernadette. *Creating a Home for Body, Soul, and Spirit: A New Approach to Childcare.* Spring Valley, NY: Waldorf Early Childhood Association of North America, 2011.

Pikler, Emmi. *Sensory Awareness Foundation Bulletin* 14 (Winter). Peterborough, NH: The Sensory Awareness Foundation, 1994.

Ris, Margaret and Trice Atchison, eds. *A Warm and Gentle Welcome.* Spring Valley, NY: Waldorf Early Childhood Association of North America, 2007.

Szanto-Feder, Agnes. *Moving with Pleasure from the Beginning: The Importance of Observation in Early Childhood.* N.p.: published by the author, 2020.

Tardos, Anna. *Bringing Up and Providing Care for Infants and Toddlers in an Institution.* Budapest: Pikler-Lóczy Association, 2007.

Udo de Haes, Daniel. Translated by Nina Kuettel. *The Creative Word: The Young Child's Experience of Language and Stories.* Spring Valley, NY: Waldorf Early Childhood Association of North America, 2014.

Weber, Susan, Nancy Macalaster, and Jane Swain. *Singing and Speaking the Child into Life: Songs, Verses and Rhythmic Games for the First Three Years.* Spring Valley, NY: Waldorf Early Childhood Association of North America, 2017.

Contributors

Susan Weber is the founding director of Sophia's Hearth Family Center. She taught in the Waldorf early childhood teacher education programs at Sophia's Hearth and at Antioch University. She is recognized internationally as a leading lecturer and writer in the field of Waldorf early childhood education, most recently at the Goetheanum in Dornach, Switzerland and in Spring Valley, New York. She also led a multi-year course on birth to three in Khon Kaen, Thailand, for teachers throughout Southeast Asia. She has focused upon understanding the first three years of the child's life through Waldorf early childhood education, especially in light of the approach of the Pikler Institute.

Katherine Scharff is the director of teacher education at Sophia's Hearth. She taught preschool and was a parent-child teacher at the Waldorf School of Saratoga Springs, New York. She is also a Simplicity Parenting family life coach. Katherine has completed the Sophia's Hearth full Waldorf teacher education program and additional training in the Pikler approach, and is a registered nurse with specialized training in the anthroposophical approach.

Jane Swain is a pediatric physical therapist and registered movement therapist. She is an associate director of the Early Childhood Teacher Education Center at Sophia's Heath in Keene, New Hampshire, and a core faculty member there. She is also a Senior Therapeutic Trainer at the Spacial Dynamics® Institute in Mechanicville, New York. Jane has studied at the Pikler Institute in Budapest, Hungary. She is certified in Bothmer Gymnastics, Sensory Integration Praxis Testing, and in Bobath/Neuro-Developmental Treatment for children with cerebral palsy and other neurological conditions. Jane has spent decades working with children and their parents, and consulting in classrooms. She is an international adult educator and has published in several American and international journals.

Deborah Laurin, PhD, is an early childhood consultant and mentor, and co-director of of the early childhood educator training at the West Coast Institute for studies in anthroposophy in British Columbia, Canada. She serves on the WECAN birth-to-three working group and on the scientific committee with Pikler USA®. Learning about the remarkable work of Dr. Emmi Pikler became the catalyst for her to study infant and toddler care. Her visits to Lóczy in 2014, 2016, and 2018, and participation in Pikler USA® and Budapest trainings at Pikler House® inspired an empirical study published in the *Infant Mental Health Journal* (2020) on caregiver interactions and child well-being and involvement during diapering practices in infant and toddler group care settings. She is an international presenter and is published in several journals.